DEAR LUDMIL

HAPPY

I HOPE

BEST

YOUR FRIEND FO

MARK x.

Feng Shaun

Discover Inner Peace with Shaun the Sheep

First published 2002 by Boxtree
an imprint of Pan Macmillan Ltd
Pan Macmillan, 20 New Wharf Road, London N1 9RR
Basingstoke and Oxford
Associated companies throughout the world
www.panmacmillan.com

ISBN 0 7522 1512 4

Produced under license by Aardman Animations
© and ™ Aardman/Wallace and Gromit Ltd 2002

Text © Macmillan Publishers Ltd 2002

5 7 9 8 6 4

A CIP catalogue record for this book is available from
the British Library.

Design by Dan Newman, Perfect Bound
Text by Natalie Jerome and Emma Marriott

Printed by Proost, Belgium

Feng Shaun

Discover Inner Peace with Shaun the Sheep

BOXTREE

Wear white, natural fabrics
to induce a feeling of calm
and purity

*Clutter blocks vital energy,
leading to frustration and subtle
obstacles in your life*

Spending more time in good company and less time in bad company will have a positive effect on your mental and spiritual wellbeing

*Slow, repetitive tasks are a great
way to ease an anxious mind*

LOVE—MAKING

Introduce love into your life —
it has a positive affect on your
thinking patterns and
endorphin levels

Prayer is often the only solution to certain insurmountable problems

LOOK GOOD, FEEL GREAT!

Personal grooming is essential for increasing self-esteem. Make sure you look your very best every day

Understand your cravings and addictions – they show a lack of control and cause unhappiness

One of the surest ways of soothing anxiety is through touch. An arm on a shoulder is a simple gesture that can sometimes work wonders

Even basic Tai Chi can lead to instant feelings of calm

After a hard day, there's nothing better than a good long soak to revive and refresh that tired old body

SPICE UP YOUR LOVE LIFE

Remember to take every
opportunity to inject some passion
into your relationship. It will do
wonders for body and soul

*Try not to over-react
in times of stress*

If in doubt, run away from trouble. Exercise is a great way of alleviating tension

JUST LEAVE ME ALONE!

There comes a time when you need to protect and barricade yourself from potentially stressful situations

IRRITABLE BOWEL?

If you're feeling bloated
and gassy, watch your diet.
A sore tummy is often due
to rich and fatty foods

*Make friends with new people.
Look beyond appearances and
remember, strangers are just friends
we haven't met*

EAT TO LIVE!

Eat more greenery – it's the perfect snack food for body and soul

*Dealing with anxiety in a calm,
dignified manner nourishes
your inner self*

Between four and six cups of coffee
or tea a day and you are over your
caffeine limit. Too much caffeine
can make you hyperactive

Anger is a negative emotion –
be bigger than your
enemies and forgive others
as often as you can